I Wonder Why

Creepy-Crawlies

KINGFISHER

NEW YORK

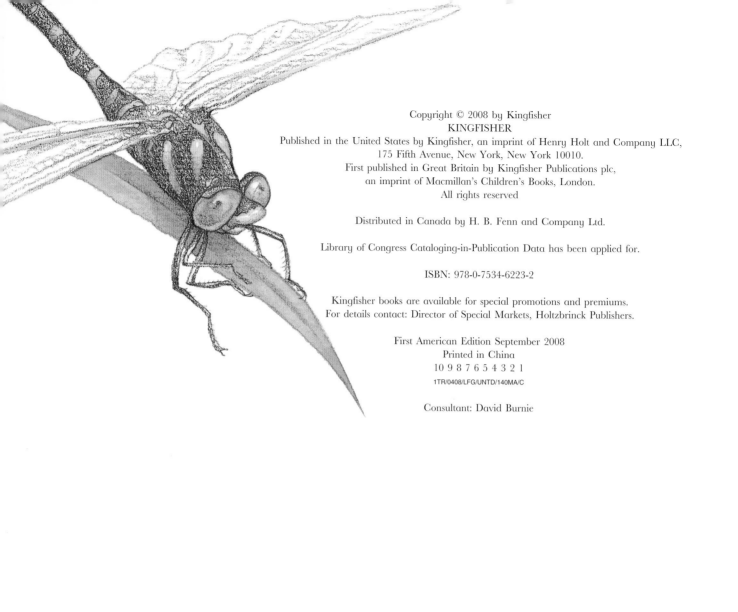

KINGFISHER
Published in the United States by Kingfisher, an imprint of Henry Holt and Company LLC,
175 Fifth Avenue, New York, New York 10010.
First published in Great Britain by Kingfisher Publications plc,
an imprint of Macmillan's Children's Books, London.

Distributed in Canada by H. B. Fenn and Company Ltd.

Library of Congress Cataloging-in-Publication Data has been applied for.

ISBN: 978-0-7534-6223-2

Kingfisher books are available for special promotions and premiums.
For details contact: Director of Special Markets, Holtzbrinck Publishers.

First American Edition September 2008
Printed in China
10 9 8 7 6 5 4 3 2 1
1TR/0408/LFG/UNTD/140MA/C

Consultant: David Burnie

Contents

What are creepy-crawlies?

Creepy-crawlies are tiny animals such as insects and spiders. They have been on Earth for millions of years and live in all types of different places, from hot, wet jungles to cold, rocky mountains.

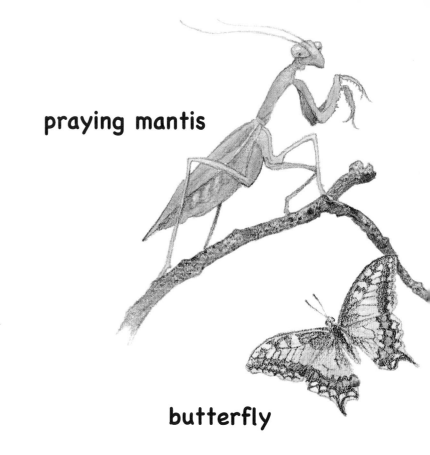

praying mantis

butterfly

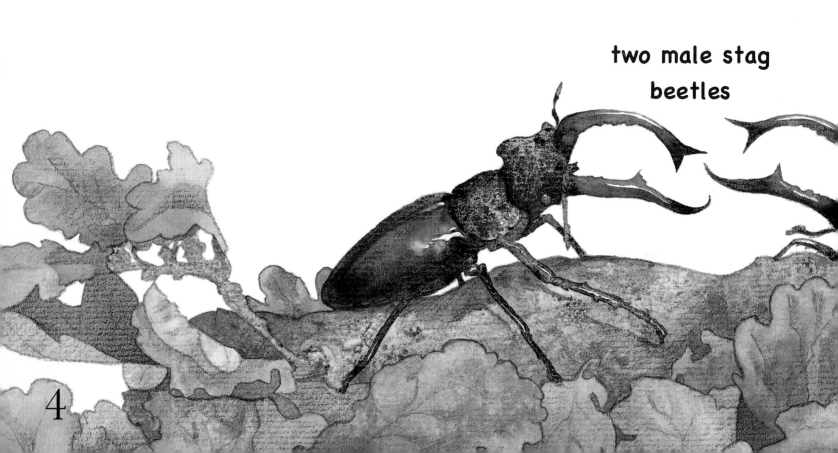

two male stag beetles

4

1. All insects have six legs. They also have three parts to their bodies—a head, thorax, and abdomen.

2. There are millions of types of insects. They come in different shapes, colors, and sizes.

3. Yes. Beetles are insects. Some are very colorful; others have huge jaws.

A stag beetle attacks another with its jaws.

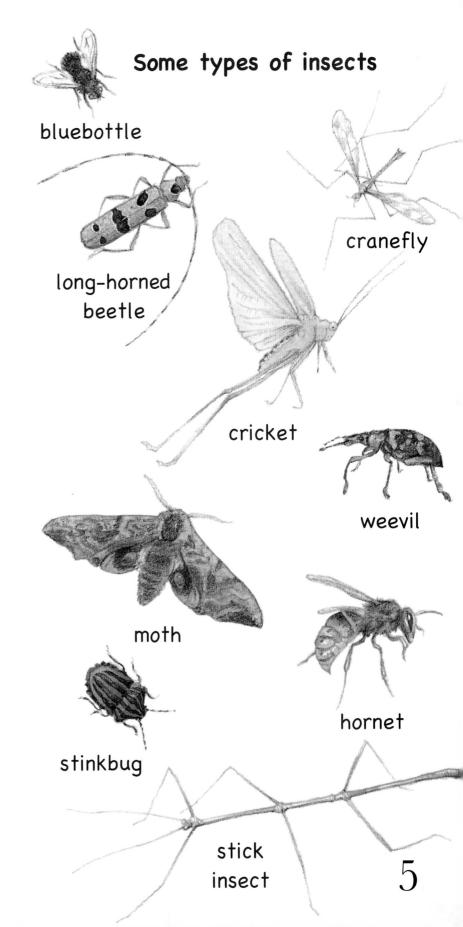

Some types of insects

bluebottle

long-horned beetle

cranefly

cricket

weevil

moth

stinkbug

hornet

stick insect

5

Ladybugs

Ladybugs are small beetles with wings. They are easy to see because they have colorful, spotted shells. Ladybugs live in gardens and meadows and have tiny mouths and a pair of jaws.

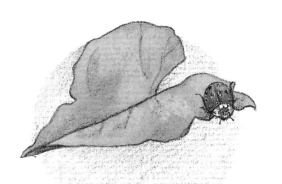

ladybug on a leaf

ladybugs on flowers

6

1. Ladybugs use their two antennae, or feelers, to touch, smell, and taste.

2. Yes. A ladybug's spotted shell is actually a hard pair of wings. They protect the softer wings underneath.

3. Ladybugs eat tiny pests that live on plants. This helps keep the plants healthy and strong.

A hungry ladybug

ladybug eating pests

7

Ants

Ants are busy insects that live in large groups. Some make their nests under stones, in the ground, or inside logs or trees. Carpenter ants, or wood ants, make their nests inside a giant pile of dead leaves.

queen ant flying

carpenter ants' nest

1. Yes. Queen ants fly away to start new nests. They lose their wings when they land.

2. Millions of ants can live in one nest. Most of these are worker ants. They take care of the queen.

3. Leafcutter ants cut up leaves with their strong jaws. Inside the nest, they use the leaves to make food.

Leafcutter ants

9

Butterflies

There are many types of butterflies. Some of them fly a long way to spend the winter in warm sunshine. Most butterflies feed on flowers. They suck up their food through their long, hollow mouth.

Becoming a butterfly

egg

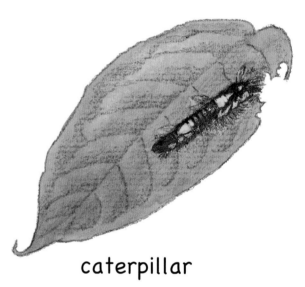

caterpillar

butterfly on a flower

mouth curled up

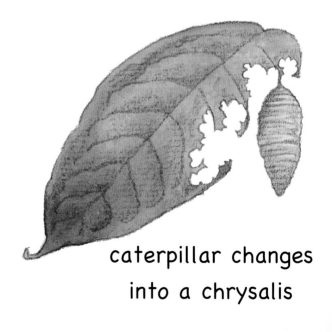

caterpillar changes into a chrysalis

10

1. Some butterflies lay one egg at a time. Others can lay hundreds of eggs on one leaf!

2. A caterpillar changes into a chrysalis, which then turns into a butterfly.

3. A monarch butterfly has strong wings. Each winter it flies thousands of miles.

Monarch butterflies flying south in the winter

Spiders

There are more than 40,000 different types of spiders. They can be smaller than the tip of a pencil or bigger than a dinner plate. All spiders can grow a new leg if one breaks.

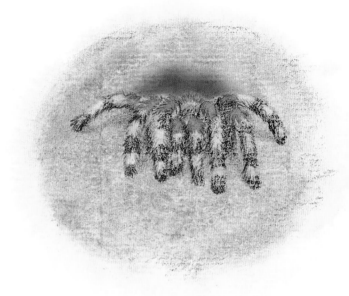

Mexican redknee tarantula

fish

1. No. Many spiders, such as this Mexican redknee tarantula, live in burrows underground.

2. A spider makes a line of silk inside its body. It sticks the silk from one place to another to build a web.

3. A water spider's long, hairy legs help the spider catch its food.

Building a web

building lines of silk

the web is finished

Honeybees

Honeybees make their nests out of wax. Inside the nest, there are thousands of small spaces, called cells. Some cells are used to store honey, and the queen bee lays her eggs in other cells.

honeybee nest

honeybees flying

14

1. Honeybees do a special dance to tell other bees in the nest where the best flowers are growing.

2. Honeybees suck nectar, a sugary water, from flowers. They turn this nectar into honey inside their bodies.

3. In the spring, a queen bee can lay more than two thousand eggs a day.

In the nest

queen honeybee laying eggs

worker honeybee feeding a grub (baby bee)

young honeybee climbing out of a cell

15

Dragonflies

Dragonflies live close to ponds and lakes. They are speedy hunters that feed on smaller insects. Some hover in the air and chase their food. Others lie in wait, snatching up insects that come too close.

dragonfly

Once dragonflies were huge.

16

1. Dragonflie
the largest
of all insec

1. Do dragonflies
have eyes?

2. Dragonflies ca
wings in differe
They can fly f
backward to es

2. Why do dragonflies
have four wings?

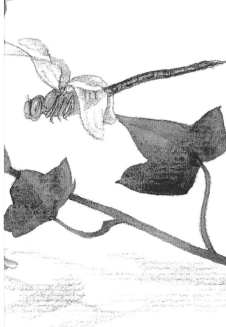

ad lying in wait

3. Dragonflies ha
Earth for 300
They were eve
before the dinc

3. How long have
dragonflies lived
on Earth?

flying backward

Index